GREAT HORNED OWL KACHINA.

THE HOPI PEOPLE

by Robert C. Euler
and Henry F. Dobyns

PUBLISHED BY INDIAN TRIBAL SERIES / PHOENIX

Library of Congress Catalog Number 79–167920

ISBN 87358–090–7

PRINTED UNITED STATES OF AMERICA · NORTHLAND PRESS

CORN IS THE BASIS of all life, an old, traditional Hopi Indian said recently. This has been the belief of these farmers of northern Arizona's high mesas for more than one thousand years of occupancy in that beautiful but semi-arid region of the Southwest. Today the Hopi are "Pueblo Indians," living in compact stone villages atop three rocky and juniper-studded mesas at the southern edge of the large and dominant Black Mesa. Their remote ancestors lived very differently.

Archaeologists have been able to identify the predecessors of the Hopi in northern Arizona back almost to the beginning of the Christian era and speak of these early people as "Kayenta Anasazi." The word *Kayenta*, after a small town on the present Navajo Indian Reservation near the Four Corners — the common juncture of the four states of Utah,

Colorado, New Mexico, and Arizona, is simply the name that archaeologists have selected for a prehistoric "tribal" group in that region. *Anasazi,* a Navajo word meaning "ancient people," represents to the archaeologist a common way of life shared by several so-called "tribes" in prehistoric times in the northern Southwest.

The earliest concrete evidence of these Hopis of the dim past comes from caves near Kayenta and in nearby regions of southern Utah and Colorado. While the earliest date for these people, whom archaeologists speak of as Basketmakers to distinguish them from later Pueblo Indians, is A.D. 217, it is obvious that their way of life was already well-established.

The caves or, more correctly, large rock-shelters in which they lived, were places where the Basketmakers could take shelter from the elements. They dug storage pits, lined with slabs of sandstone and covered with juniper bark and branches, in the natural sandy floors. They had not yet come in contact with the art of making ceramics, a technique that had long been known in southern Arizona and Mexico. As their name implies, they wove very fine baskets and flexible bags of a number of shapes and functions.

The earliest Basketmakers used the storage cists in the floors of their shelters also as burial crypts and, in the almost totally dry atmosphere, the bodies of the dead were naturally mummified. This gives archaeologists a good idea of the physical type of these early Hopi. Moreover, since it was their custom to place offerings in the graves, there are also found baskets, weapons, food, and various items of personal adornment.

The Basketmakers wore neatly woven sandals of yucca fiber, loincloths of other natural plant fibers, and, in cold winter months, warm robes of strips of rabbit fur tied together.

EARLY EXISTENCE

Although it may seem incredible to the modern traveler whisking his way along paved highways within a few hundred yards of some of the Basketmaker caves, these ancient Indians led a relatively comfortable existence. In nearby valleys they farmed corn and squash in such abundance that they were not only able to store quantities for future use, but also to preserve the best seeds for planting. They also gathered wild vegetal products such as piñon nuts, acorns, cactus fruits, and sunflower seeds. Meat was probably important in their diet also and large quantities of animal bones are found in their refuse. They ate deer, mountain sheep, rabbits, badgers, and many smaller animals. They hunted with a spear and a spear thrower or snared their prey in large knotted nets; the bow and arrow was as yet unknown to them.

They had no domestic animals except the dog from whose hair they wove beautiful belts and sashes. These animals were probably kept primarily as pets.

Some time around A.D. 500, gradual changes took place in the lives of these Indians. They learned to construct pithouses, shallow rounded depressions in the ground with walls of stone slabs and roofs of poles and brush covered with mud. Most of these houses were out in the open and congregated into small villages, presaging perhaps a more nucleated social community.

During this period, called the "Modified Basketmaker," the Indians learned how to make and fire true pottery. Ceramic vessels were often started in a basket and then coiled, each coil or roll of clay being made to adhere to the one beneath and obliterated by a scraping process. The use of the potter's wheel was unknown in the prehistoric New World, so all of this work was carried out by hand. When the vessels were dry they were sometimes painted with simple designs in black organic paint and then fired in a wood fire. Since oxygen was not allowed to circulate freely around the pot, the resultant color was usually some shade of gray, although occasionally red vessels are uncovered. At the same time, many fine baskets continued to be produced.

New varieties of corn and squash were planted and some time during this period the common kidney bean was introduced to these farmers. Certainly this added a measurable amount of protein to their diet.

The bow and arrow also came into use and this probably increased the amount of game that the Basketmakers were able to procure.

In all, these were important years for they provided the base upon which the later great development of Hopi civilization was built.

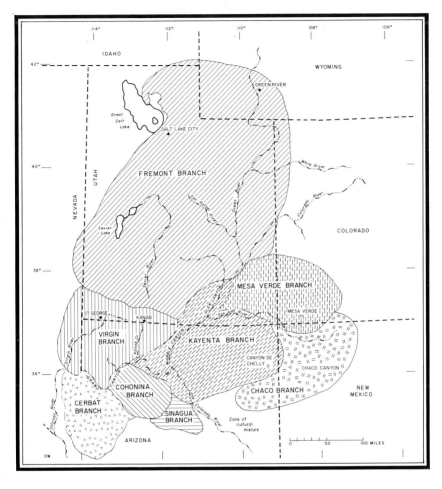

THE KAYENTA BRANCH of the Anasazi cultural tradition, ancestral to the Hopi, and its neighboring prehistoric cultures.

By A.D. 700 or 800 other developments took place, among them, in certain areas, the move to surface houses of crude masonry or of poles set on end and plastered with mud. The rooms of these houses often adjoined one another and formed roughly L-shaped structures. The earlier pithouses, however, were not completely abandoned, but often served as ceremonial chambers, the forerunner of the *kiva,* or underground religious room of the Hopis of today. From this period on, these Indians are referred to as "Pueblos," from the Spanish word for contiguous-room adobe or masonry villages. Later in this "Developmental Pueblo" period, the Indians better learned their stone masons' trade and constructed very serviceable "apartment houses," often in the shape of a U, sometimes of two stories, and usually with a subterranean *kiva* in front.

While the art of basketmaking tended to decline, specialization occurred in ceramics. Much better pottery was made of more different types. The Kayenta Anasazi produced redwares and white vessels, both painted with black designs. On the cooking vessels, they often left coils unobliterated, producing the common gray "corrugated" ware of the time.

These people added cotton to the list of cultivated plants and the turkey to the domesticated animal roster. Again, however, there is no evidence that this great American bird was eaten; rather, its feathers were incorporated into cloaks and the live birds

7

themselves may have been used in ceremonies. The cotton was spun and woven on looms.

Prehistorians infer that the domesticated turkeys testify to cultural influences reaching these aborigines from the early civilizations of Middle America. In fact, the Mexican variety of domestic turkey found carefully buried in Kayenta sites constitutes firm evidence of trade relationships between the local Indians and members of more complex societies farther south. While evidence is not clear as to what the northern natives bartered for Mexican turkeys, it is possible that Indian mining began at this early date in order to extract turquoise to exchange for the turkeys whose feathers were evidently regarded as essential for certain ritual actions.

The Pueblos supplemented their diet of corn, beans, and squash with many wild foods and continued to hunt a large number of both large and small animals.

Survivors usually buried the dead with the knees tightly flexed, in pits dug in the refuse. They placed offerings in the graves, usually in the form of pottery bowls and jars.

TRANSITIONAL PERIOD

This was certainly a time of transition for the Pueblo Indians. They changed their house styles, developed the form of their *kivas*, improved their pottery, added axes, hoes and the loom to their technological inventory, and cotton in their fields.

The Anasazi culture perhaps reached the peak of

8

its development between the 11th and 14th centuries, A.D. Before 1300, large communities of open sites and cliff dwellings had been built in the Kayenta region as well as in other areas of the Pueblo domain. Some of these were four and even five stories in height and contained hundreds of rooms; often many *kivas* were associated with each village.

Growing surpluses of foods, the Pueblos had leisure to develop religion and the arts. With increased "urbanization," changes surely occurred in the social and political structure of these Indians.

One index of changing religion and social structure was again the importation from the south of bird feathers for ritual purposes. Beginning sometime after about A.D. 900, the Pueblo Indians began to incorporate into their ceremonial costumes the brightly colored feathers of tropical macaws and parrots. Pueblo traders not only imported the feathers, but also live birds which were then kept in captivity in rooms in the pueblos. Apparently ritual leaders plucked the long, brilliantly-hued tail and wing feathers from these captive birds as required for ceremonial usage, and probably kept the birds alive as long as possible. In any event, when such birds died or were ritually killed, religious functionaries reverently interred their bodies under the floors of special pueblo rooms, providing later excavators with direct evidence of the parrot trade between the ancestors of the Hopi and civilized Middle Americans.

In the last quarter of the 13th century, the Kayenta region climate changed. Archaeologists find

9

evidence that the streams upon which the Pueblos depended for their crops cut deeply into the sandy soil. Some areas were subjected to extreme drought conditions. There is some evidence that "foreign" Indians appeared on the northern horizons of Kayenta territory. For these, and probably other reasons as well, these Anasazi abandoned much of their far-flung homeland. Most of them seem to have gone south, to the southern edges of Black Mesa where, with a more dependable water supply available, they built some of the largest villages in their long history. These lie today in ruins on the Hopi Reservation, most waiting for the shovel and trowel of the archaeologist to reveal the history of their inhabitants.

A few have been excavated, however, most notably the great site of Awatovi, whose span of occupation bridges from prehistoric to historic times for the Hopi. Here, and in numerous nearby villages, the Pueblo people continued to develop their cultural patterns. The same crops were grown, the same animals hunted, the same wild plants collected.

There are some indications by A.D. 1300 that the Hopi were in more direct contact with other Pueblo or Pueblo-like peoples to the south and southeast, below the Little Colorado River.

In the upper stretches of that drainage, between the Hopi and the Zuñi, the form of the *kiva* changed from circular to rectangular, and this was soon adopted by both Pueblo groups. The walls of these *kivas* were often decorated with murals of painted geometric and other designs.

Photograph by George H. Pepper   *Courtesy Museum of the American Indian*

HOPI SNAKE PRIEST photographed in 1897 in front of the First Mesa village of Walpi.

It was at this time, too, that the ceramic art of the Hopi changed to its present form. No longer were pottery vessels of a black-on-white or black-on-red variety made. Using the natural deposits of coal that were exposed near their villages (incidentally, a domestic use of coal that came much earlier for the Hopi than for Europeans), they fired their bowls and jars in a much higher temperature than it had been possible to achieve earlier. Although experimentation with coal-fired pottery had occurred much earlier on Black Mesa, by A.D. 1300 almost all Hopi wares were so fired. This produced a beautiful pale yellow luster that potters enhanced with often elaborate designs, including a number of life forms, painted in a brownish-black.

TRADE

Many Indians other than Hopis highly prized this Jeddito Ware, as prehistorians term it. Hopi traders distributed this commodity widely over the Colorado Plateau and beyond for many decades. Bits of broken Jeddito vessels turn up far to the west in California.

Hopi handwoven textiles from the men's looms in their *kivas* quite clearly commanded an excellent return in inter-tribal trade, where they enjoyed great demand. Textile production from the *kivas* constituting a surplus beyond immediate clan requirements furnished Hopi traders with highly valued goods to carry over the trails to sources of Hopi imports.

The Hopi people possessed a taste for the sweet roasted heart of the *Agave* or "century plant," so they carried on a fairly brisk trade in the dried food produced by the less sedentary Pai Indians to the west. The Hopis bartered both Jeddito Yellow ware vessels and cotton blankets for the relished sweet.

The Hopis also obtained non-food trade goods from the Northeastern Pai. The latter mined red ochre pigment from a cave deposit in their territory that Hopis obtained both for their own use and to trade eastward to other Pueblo Indians at a high markup.

Hopi and Pai trading partners dealt as middleman, moreover, in long-distance inter-tribal commerce in Pacific Coast seashells, involving lower Colorado River Mojaves and Halchidhoma. The Hopi themselves generated significant demand for abalone and other shells to be used in performing a number of their own religious rituals. They also traded shells eastward to other Pueblos requiring them for similar ceremonial purposes, making the same sort of middleman's profit they took on red ochre.

At the beginning of the 16th century, the Hopis also apparently still traded directly with the northern Piman-speaking Indians on the Gila River and south of it. Parrots and macaws and their brilliantly colored feathers to complete ceremonial costumes appear to have constituted the most valuable goods exchanged northward to the Hopis.

ABORIGINAL HOPI SOCIETY

While the Hopis carried on a lively and large-scale trade with many other tribesmen, these Indians developed their own distinctive pattern of social organization and religious life. Here we summarize our reconstruction of those patterns at about 1500 A.D.

To begin with maize, that conceptual basis for Hopi life, the agricultural fields where it grew belonged by Hopi law to clans dominated by women. The maize and other harvests likewise belonged to women who controlled household life, dispensing food and other resources to sons and husbands.

The Hopi household itself fell under the sway of senior women who owned the houses. Thus, a Hopi man moved from his mother's home upon marriage to take up residence in his bride's household. Each household included several closely related women led and very largely controlled by a matriarch. That matriarch was usually the eldest woman of her lineage, reckoned through the female line. If a matriarch and her sisters and their daughters with their husbands overcrowded a single dwelling, they set up housekeeping in adjacent rooms within the village. A man whose wife died moved back to the household of his mother or sister. Hopi residence followed, therefore, a "matrilocal" pattern, because women lived with or nearby their mothers while men moved to their wives' homes.

Several Hopi households inhabited by matrilineages of the sort just described constituted a matrilineal clan when they all traced their descent from the same female ancestor. The Hopi people regarded one specific household in each clan as the ancestral one for that clan, so that its matriarch served as Clan Mother. This matriarch's brother acted as that clan's ceremonial leader, since Hopi men spent a good deal of time carrying out clan rituals as well as male secret society ceremonies.

The Hopi men and their sons — who belonged to their mother's clan — hunted, cut and hauled timber and coal for fuel, and cultivated the sand dunes and flood-watered fields. They also patrolled the environs of the Hopi settlements to intercept and turn back hostile raiders.

The women and girls who made up the social core of the matrilineage household cooperatively kept house. They stored and processed and cooked all food for themselves and their husbands and sons. These women carried drinking and cooking water from the springs and tended the tiny kitchen gardens that often had to be hand-watered. They wove baskets and fashioned the clay vessels that played an important economic role in intertribal trade. As a matter of course, the women cared for all the infants and young children not yet helping with chores.

Members of every Hopi clan felt themselves to be especially related to a *wuya*, either an animal such as the bear, or a plant such as the reed, or a weapon such as the bow, or a natural phenomenon such as a cloud, or a supernatural concept such as the Sun's Forehead. A Hopi clan took its name from its *wuya*, which clan members believed imbued it with a special quality and provided it with protection. Each clan kept a fetish representation of its *wuya* in its ancestral clan house.

Hopi clans maintained proper reciprocal relation-

Photograph by John Griffin

MISHONGNOVI KIVA with the sacred San Francisco Peaks in the distant background. The San Francisco Peaks are thought to be the home of most Hopi kachinas.

ships with the supernatural by ardently performing religious rituals for which they were responsible. The proprietary clan for each ceremonial furnished a chief priest of the secret ceremonial society whose members conducted one of the calendrical rituals scheduled throughout the year.

Hopi men conducted their main rituals between the winter and summer solstices when their horticultural workload was lightest. They carried out rituals demanding less time between summer and winter solstices when they were busy cultivating and harvesting the fundamental crop of maize and its various horticultural supplements.

Thus, the Hopi ceremonial calendar opened with a Winter Solstice ritual symbolically expressing the world view stressing reciprocity and interdependence, fertility and the Hopi Emergence and migration.

The second ritual in the annual sequence was the "Bean Dance" performed by the Powamu Society. This symbolized Hopi preparations for the coming horticultural season of maize and other crop growth. Boys and girls also passed through their initiation into Hopi ceremonial life during this ritual every fourth year.

The third, or Niman ritual in mid-summer marked the termination of the major ceremonial cycle, and emphasized the maturation of maize and the other growing crops. About a month later, the Flute or Snake–Antelope rituals sought weather control, particularly rain-bringing to provide the growing maize and supplemental plantings sufficient moisture to mature and ripen. The Hopis regarded the snakes the priests collected and handled during these rites as messengers to carry the message of their need for moisture to the supernatural beings dispensing that life-giving fluid.

The fourth major Hopi calendrical ritual occurred perhaps a month prior to the winter solstice. During this Wuwuchim or "Grown Man" ritual period, the villagers shut off the trails leading into their settlements. Like the Aztecs far to the south, the Hopi at this time extinguished all of their fires. Then, while women and children hid indoors, a chief priest kindled a new fire to be carried into the kiva ceremonial chambers and dwellings. From time to time, the ceremonial leaders initiated young men into full adult status during this rite.

While the Hopi men conducted much of this ritual cycle out in the open, the secret societies truly kept much of the ceremony from women and uninitiated youths. They did so by constructing underground ceremonial chambers termed *kivas*. These could be entered only by a ladder through a small hole in the roof. Hopi artists painted religious scenes on the white-plastered walls of many *kivas* and their builders carefully fitted them with benches, draft deflectors, fire pits, resonating chambers in the floor, and loom attachments in roof beams and floor as well as niches in the walls for storing ritual paraphernalia. Besides serving as a ceremonial chamber for secret religious rites, the *kivas* also provided Hopi men with a sort of masculine retreat from

20

female-dominated households. Even the *kiva* afforded Hopi men only a limited refuge from the female organizing principle of Hopi life, however, since women did join in a number of *kiva* functions. Even when men were alone in the *kivas* they necessarily spent much time working at their looms, for they had not only to weave the precious Hopi textiles that earned foreign exchange in terms of turkeys, parrots, dried *agave* pulp, and so on, but first they had to weave basic apparel for their wives, sisters, mothers, and daughters and themselves.

Anthropological linguists classify the tongue Hopis speak as belonging to the Shoshonean branch of the Uto–Aztecan. In other words, Hopi is related to the speech of Utes and Paiutes to the north, but they cannot understand it. Hopi is even more remotely aligned with the Nahuatl language of the Aztecs. More important to an understanding of the Hopi people than the classification of their language is how it frames their cultural perceptions and binds them to a particular world view emanating from their language patterns.

To give one example, the past-present-future orientation that English imposes on its speakers is lacking in Hopi grammar. So much do English speakers take this as a matter of course that they find it incomprehensible that those speaking another language can phrase thoughts about time without it. Yet the English concept of time is nearly incomprehensible to Hopis. Their "validity-forms" reflect upon the speaker rather than the subject. A Hopi reports something happening (the English past and present) or that he expects to happen (the English future). Hopi verb "aspects" express varying duration, while "clause-linkage" enables Hopis to indicate whether an event took place sooner or later than another. While this seems complicated to a non-Hopi speaker, it makes it simple to distinguish between momentary, continued and repeated occurrences, as well as to mark a precise sequence of events.

THE COMING OF THE SPANIARDS

Unknown to the industrious Hopis, zealously pursuing their annual cycle of ceremonies, inwardly to maintain reciprocity between the natural and supernatural worlds, and outwardly carrying on their economic trading relationships, the natural world was more complex than they could possibly know. Their millennium-long struggle to survive in an environment that was no better than marginal for sedentary horticulturists would soon be complicated by another ethnic group with a metal technology and strong beliefs in one jealous God.

In the spring of 1539, just twenty years after the Spaniards landed in force on the American continent, the Viceroy of New Spain, Antonio de Mendoza, dispatched a small exploring party northward from the colonial frontier in Sinaloa to attempt to authenticate rumors of "heathen" Indians inhabiting golden cities to the north. Leading the expedition was Franciscan friar Marcos de Niza. With him, a Moorish slave named Estevan and a sizeable group of Mexican Indians traveled north through Sonora into what is now Arizona. Estevan and some of the Indians, moving ahead of Marcos by several days, apparently reached one of the Zuñi pueblos, constructed of stone and sun-dried bricks and not the legendary gold. There the natives killed Estevan, and Friar Marcos, not wishing to continue alone as the Indians deserted him, returned to Culiacan and made his report to the governor of the province, Francisco Vasquez de Coronado.

This report, although probably accurate enough, was misinterpreted, and the thoughts of accumulating gold and precious turquoise to bolster a faltering economy in Spain, as well as converts to Christianity, really set New Spain aflame with excitement.

Mendoza selected Vasquez de Coronado to lead a sizeable army and exploring expedition back to the north. The mounted column reached the Zuñi area, which the Spaniards called Cibola, without incident. The first pueblo sighted was Hawikuh, probably the one in which Estevan had been put to death. The Indians refused to submit to Coronado, whereupon the Spaniards attacked and captured the town within an hour.

At Hawikuh the Spanish commander first learned of similar Indians to the northwest in a province called Tusayan. These were, of course, the Hopi and it is quite probable that even though they had not yet seen a Spaniard, they had heard of their hostile arrival at Zuñi.

Vasquez de Coronado promptly dispatched one of

his lieutenants, Don Pedro de Tovar, the Franciscan friar Juan de Padilla, seventeen horsemen and three or four foot soldiers to explore the province of Tusayan. In mid-July of 1540, the small party reached what probably was the Hopi village of Kawiokuh on the easternmost of the four occupied mesas. Approaching the town at night, they went undetected by the inhabitants. So dramatic was the first meeting of Hopis and Europeans the following morning that it seems best to relate it in the words of Castañeda, the official chronicler for the Coronado Expedition. Castañeda wrote:

"But in the morning they were discovered and drew up in regular order, while the natives came out to meet them, with bows, and shields, and wooden clubs, drawn up in lines without any confusion. The interpreter was given a chance to speak to them and give them due warning, for they were very intelligent people, but nevertheless they drew lines and insisted that our men should not go across these lines toward their village. While they were talking, some men acted as if they would cross the lines, and one of the natives lost control of himself and struck a horse a blow on the cheek of the bridle with his club. Friar Juan, fretted by the time that was being wasted talking with them, said to the captain: 'To tell the truth, I do not know why we came here.' When the men heard this, they gave the Santiago [battle cry] so suddenly that they ran down many Indians and the others fled to the town in confusion. Some indeed did not have a chance to

HOPI MAN wearing breechcloth, moccasins and headband, weaving a blanket on a native-style loom stretched between the roof beams and floor niches of a kiva.

do this, so quickly did the people in the village come out with presents, asking for peace. The captain ordered his force to collect, and as the natives did not do any more harm, he and those who were with him found a place to establish their headquarters near the village. They had dismounted here when the natives came peacefully, saying that they had come to give in the submission of the whole province and that they wanted him to be friends with them and to accept the presents which they gave him. This was some cotton cloth, although not much, because they do not make it in that district. They also gave him some dressed skins and corn meal, and pine nuts and corn and birds of the country. Afterward they presented some turquoises, but not many. The people of the whole district came together that day and submitted themselves, and they allowed him to enter their villages freely to visit, buy, sell, and barter with them.

It is governed like Cibola, by an assembly of the oldest men. They have their governors and generals. This was where they obtained the information about a large river, and that several days down the river there were some people with very large bodies."

Thus, on that fateful, hot summer day in July of 1540, the historic period opened for the Hopi. For more than a century thereafter it was to be one of hardship and frustration for these sedentary planters of corn.

The report of the "large river" given to Tovar by the Hopis soon brought another small expedition of Spaniards. After Tovar's return to Zuñi, Vasquez de Coronado dispatched another of his lieutenants, Don Garcia Lopez de Cardenas with twelve companions to locate this river. They were well received by the Hopis who provided guides for the remainder of the journey. After a trip of twenty days (which may be an exaggeration of Castañeda), they came to the rim of a great gorge into which they tried but were unable to descend. This, undoubtedly, was the first sighting of Grand Canyon by Europeans.

The Hopi abandoned the village of Kawiokuh after that initial encounter, along with several others on that eastern mesa. At least they were falling into ruin by the time the next Spanish *entrada*, commanded by Antonio de Espejo, reached them in 1583. With Friar Bernardino Beltran and 14 soldiers, Espejo had come north to New Mexico to learn the fate of three priests who had been left in one of the pueblos along the Rio Grande by the Spanish military explorer Francisco Sanchez Chamuscado a year earlier. Although Espejo learned that the three fathers had been martyred, he persevered in what, under the circumstances, was one of the most remarkable feats of exploration in Southwestern history. With his small party he accomplished as much exploration in Arizona and New Mexico as had Vasquez de Coronado with his great army. Although the entire country was seething with hostility towards the Spaniards, Espejo visited a number of pueblos, including the Hopi, and located several valuable mines before returning to Mexico in the fall of 1583. Espejo found the Hopis living in five villages. Apparently with an ability to win the friendship of the Hopis, he received a hospitable welcome and the Indians furnished him with guides for his search for mineral wealth.

The people of Awatovi offered Espejo's men different gifts from those reportedly presented to Tovar forty-three years earlier. The differences may reflect a new Hopi strategy for placating Spaniards, economic shifts during the interval between explorations, or other changes. In 1583, Awatovi inundated the explorers with food and clothing: venison, dried rabbit meat, maize, roasting ears, ground maize meal and tamales plus firewood with which to cook and six hundred cotton blankets, both pure white and ornamented. Conspicuously missing from the 1583 goods offered were the birds, dressed skins (very likely imports from the Northeastern Pai Indians) and turquoise of 1540. The Hopis clearly impressed the chronicler of the 1583 expedition with the quantity of cotton cloth presented, while his 1540 counterpart mentioned only "some cotton cloth." On the other hand, the 1540 "gifts" reportedly included only pinyon nuts and corn meal, in contrast to the range of foodstuffs provided in 1583.

Possibly 1583 was simply a poor pinyon harvest year. Possibly the Hopis remembered that the Spaniards did not know how to extract the tasty nuts from their shells in 1540. Possibly Espejo's expedition luckily visited Awatovi when a very large stock of trade blankets had accumulated, or perhaps native textile production taken for granted in 1530 loomed large by 1583.

Near the end of the 16th century, in 1598 to be precise, another Spanish explorer and colonizer traveled from the Rio Grande to the Hopi towns. This was Don Juan de Oñate who, with 400 men (130 of whom had families with them), 83 wagons, and several thousand cattle, established Spain's first settlement in New Mexico, north of the present city of Santa Fe. Oñate found the Hopis without resistance and received from them formal submission to the King of Spain. He later assigned two missionaries to the Hopi but the assignments were never begun.

Parenthetically, two Hopis were to have a grim encounter with Spanish brutality at the hands of Oñate's men in the following year. Apparently these two were visiting in the New Mexico pueblo of Acoma when Oñate attacked that village in an attempt to punish the Indians for having killed one of his lieutenants. The Hopis were among the prisoners taken and, before they were allowed to return to their own villages, were each sentenced to have their right hands cut off.

For the next twenty-five years the Spaniards made only sporadic visits to the Hopi. Oñate returned in 1604 on his way to explore the Gulf of Lower California. In 1614, a Captain Marquez with 25 soldiers noted that the five Hopi villages still occupied had a total population of about 3,000.

THE CONVERSION PROGRAM

Finally, in 1628, the Franciscans decided to begin their conversion program in earnest, and three priests were assigned to the Hopis. In spite of previous ill treatment at the hands of the Europeans, the Hopis cooperated and in actuality built three mission churches. Within a few years, churches had been constructed at Awatovi, the only village still occupied on the eastern mesa, at Shungopovi just below the modern village of the same name, and, farther to the west at Oraibi. There were also two outliers, *visitas,* to these last two churches, one at Walpi and one at Mishongnovi, both below the present mesa-top villages of those names. By 1630, one Spanish priest claimed that there were 10,000 Hopis and that he was converting them rapidly.

As the Hopis helped to build Roman Catholic mission churches and priests' quarters, they incorporated into these structures some materials imported over a trade caravan route extending all the way south to Mexico City. Every three years, at least in theory, Franciscan administrators loaded large wagon trains with the robes and vestments, the religious vessels and utensils, and even the building materials, that the missionaries in the Custodia of New Mexico would require for a three-year period. Mission subsidies from the royal treasury paid for these purchases in Mexico City or nearby cities, so that little money actually circulated in New Mexico for many decades.

The Hopi mission establishments boasted bells to ring to call converts to Mass and other sacraments. Altar stones containing holy relics came to these missions over the long caravan route. Probably most if not all of the metal utilized in Hopi mission work of church construction came from the supply wagons — door and window hinges, locks, nails, latches, as well as wood-working tools such as hammers, crowbars, adzes, saws, chisels, augers, and planes. The missionaries even freighted in cordage, although serviceable cords and ropes could be woven locally from yucca and *agave* fiber, cotton, wool and even human hair.

Adept Hopi traders converted Spanish manufactured goods into profitable items of trade to other Indians not directly in contact with the Spaniards. Meeting the westernmost Northeastern Pai Indians for the first time in mid–1776, for example, Friar Francisco Garces noted that they wore leather belts of Spanish style with metal buckles obtained from the Hopis. By trading manufactured goods westward, the Hopis could insure their continued supply of the wild food products they relished, such as dried *agave* pulp, as well as Pacific coast seashells important in native religious ritual.

Signs of Hopi resistance to their Spanish conquerors appeared almost simultaneously with the founding of Roman Catholic missions at three of the towns. The missionary at Awatovi, Father Francisco Porras, whose initial impact clearly set in motion a widening factional divergence between Awatovi and other Hopis, died in 1633, reportedly poisoned by older men, perhaps native secret religious society priests.

In 1650, some Hopis journeyed to the distant Spanish provincial capital in Santa Fe to denounce a later missionary, Salvador de Guerra, for his cruel treatment of the Indians. It seems that Guerra had accused a Hopi, probably a native priest engaged in his own religious activities, of "an act of idolatry." For this, Guerra had the man bloodily whipped in public and again inside the church. Finally, this man of God covered the poor Indian with turpentine and set him afire. Although Guerra was soon removed from the Hopi country, other Spanish missionaries stayed, and managed an uneventful record of baptism as well as of teaching some Hopis how to read and write. It is probable also that during these years the Spaniards imposed upon Hopi towns the Spanish village political organization. Certainly, this superimposition of the Spanish over the Hopi took a physical form. In order to show the "heathens" the superiority of the Spanish church, their altars were often placed directly over the native religious *kivas* of the Indians.

THE PUEBLO REVOLT OF 1680

Similar "conversion" techniques were being used by the Spaniards in the New Mexico Pueblos, and by August of 1680, these village-dwelling Indians had

had enough. For the only time in their history, all of the Pueblo Indians rose in a concerted revolt against the Europeans. The Hopi formed an integral part of the rebellion, and almost immediately killed the four Spanish priests residing in their villages.

The Pueblo Revolt forced the Spaniards to abandon New Mexico and retreat to modern Ciudad Juarez–El Paso on the Texas–Chihuahua border. After one governor failed in an attempted reconquest, Diego de Vargas effectively reconquered the New Mexico Pueblos in 1692, although smaller-scale revolts in 1693 and 1696 kept Spanish rule shaky for several more years. Hopi participation in the Pueblo Revolt ended Spanish Christian missionary residence in Hopi settlements, however, for Hopis successfully resisted later Spanish attempts to re-assert colonial authority in Tusayan Province. As a Hopi might view the matter, the defeat of the Christian God by the native supernaturals in 1680 became permanent.

One Hopi leader seems to have played an outstanding role in planning and executing the revolt in the Hopi villages, and later in defeating relatively weak Spanish attempts to reimpose colonial rule and missionary residence. Called Francisco de Espeleta in Spanish reports, this Hopi took his Spanish name from the Franciscan missionary Jose de Espeleta, who taught his namesake to read and write. Certainly the Hopi Espeleta must have learned a great deal more — enough to make him successful both in organizing Hopi-refugee military forces and out-negotiating the Spaniards bent upon reconquest.

ELDERLY HOPI MATRON photographed about 1890 with native hand woven dress and sash shelling corn in yucca sifter basket.

While strong individual leadership seemed anti-thetical to Hopi ideals and social structure, Spanish documents identify the Hopi Espeleta as the main post-revolt leader of the Hopi and Pueblo refugee forces denying them any foothold on the mesas. Incorporation of recalcitrant refugees into the Hopi homeland and military forces perhaps best testifies to Espeleta's planning and organizational ability. The effective utilization of refugee forces to prevent Spanish reconquest of the Tusayan Province seems too well executed to appear merely accidental or fortuitous.

Refugees from the New Mexico Pueblos apparently already resided among the Hopis by the time de Vargas showed the royal standard in Tusayan in 1692. While the various Pueblo populations had long sought refuge in one another's settlements in periods of drought and famine, the migration of refugees to Hopi country at the end of the Seventeenth Century was incomparably larger than any other such movement since the wholesale relocation of Pueblo settlements during and after the Great Drought of 1276–1299. Moreover, the circumstances of the political refugee following 1680 differed from those of adjustments to environmental stress. Allowing refugees to settle in Hopi territory and exploit Hopi resources implies Hopi recognition of and planning for the threat of Spanish military reconquest.

Spanish records of refugee resettlement in New Mexico during the 18th century identify contingents from at least the Pueblos of Isleta, Sandia, Pajarito,

Alameda and evidently various Tewa-speaking Pueblos. The latter settled permanently on First Mesa where they remain to this day. The Sandia people later were persuaded to return to the Rio Grande, as were those from Isleta, Pajarito and Alameda.

The Tusayan Province became a refuge area for New Mexico Pueblo families, and perhaps whole clans, that wished to escape Spanish colonial rule in the aftermath of the Pueblo Revolt of 1680. While many Pueblo settlements had previously offered refuge to other Pueblo villagers in times of environmental crisis, the Hopis after 1680 offered refuge from political stress. It seems doubtful that any Pueblos had confederated to cope with earlier natural disasters. Yet the Hopi towns formed a league to incorporate Pueblo political refugees into their own politico-military alliance. The successful military and economic cooperation between the various Hopi settlements relocated to strong defensive sites on mesa margins and refugee New Mexico Pueblos which erected new towns on the Hopi mesas, contrasted markedly with the disintegration of inter-Pueblo political and military cooperation in New Mexico that occurred even before de Vargas marched north in 1692. The Hopis not merely granted asylum, they actively integrated the New Mexico refugees into the strongest post-Pueblo Revolt military force that the natives maintained following the initial uprising.

The question arises whether the Hopi leaders did

not deliberately plan permanent military resistance to Spanish colonialism. It seems highly likely that the Hopis actually invited the most recalcitrant of the New Mexico Pueblo peoples to join forces with them in their relatively remote location in order to increase the size of the military force available to fight off expectable Spanish columns. Moreover, in view of the outstanding leadership of the Hopi Espeleta that emerges dimly from Spanish records, the question also arises whether he supplied the strategic thinking and comprehension of Spanish behavior that led to creating the Hopi inter-village and refugee military alliance.

Hopi skill at bluffing Spanish commanders during the century following the Pueblo Revolt stands out in the surviving documents. The reluctance of Spanish field commanders to commit troops to a full-fledged test of military power in Hopi country was marked, even though no Spanish officer ever dared to state openly such reluctance. The reality appears to have been that Spanish forces operating at the end of an always overextended supply line in the Hopi country actually faced native forces so numerous as to make the outcome of a fire-fight doubtful. The Hopi inter-village alliance that included the refugee settlements achieved critical numerical superiority over the forces the Spanish colonial authorities could bring to bear. That alliance stands, therefore, as an enduring monument to the Hopi leadership during and following the 1680 Revolt. As far as the Spaniards could discern, the Hopi Espeleta played surely a key role, and evidently the primary role, in that leadership, as the architect of permanent autonomy.

The Hopis and refugees rendered formal obeisance to Vargas in 1692 but observed the letter more than the spirit of their supposed reincorporation into the Spanish empire. Vargas, in turn, made a show of force, but did not even go to Oraibi, largest of the Hopi settlements.

The Hopis permitted missionaries to visit their towns and preach from time to time. Yet when two Franciscans whom the Spaniards themselves described as "carried away by" their "apostolic zeal" spent several days at Awatovi in 1700, Espeleta mobilized 800 warriors to threaten the priests and rough them up. He did not commit the strategic error of 1680 by killing the missionaries, which would surely have called for strong Spanish reprisal. Bullying the priests with 800 men without harming them undoubtedly required command control of a very high order, indeed.

Espeleta allowed the missionaries several days of reconversion so successful that they left to make preparations for re-establishing the Awatovi mission. Once they departed safely, Espeleta attacked Awatovi with reportedly only 100 men, executed the males and distributed the women and children to other settlements, thus laying the foundation for matrilineal clan claims to lands in the Antelope Mesa area even today.

The Hopi Espeleta must be regarded, on available

evidence, as by far the most successful Indian leader of the great Pueblo Revolt. Not until 1716 did a Spanish commander report dealing with a Hopi leadership group, after Espeleta's death. Not until 1742 did a Spanish missionary report success in luring refugees back to New Mexico, signaling the beginning of the decline of the Hopi-refugee alliance. Not until 1870 did Christian missionaries again take up residence among the Hopis, and that occurred under a much more powerful empire than Spain's.

As a socio-religious movement back to the "good old days" before Spanish domination, the Pueblo Revolt of 1680 achieved only a temporary success of twelve years of independence. The conservative Pueblo priests who forged a temporary union that forced the Spaniards out of New Mexico proved unable to continue their cooperation. On the other hand, the Hopi Espeleta organized a resistance that achieved independence for very nearly 200 years! Dimly as scanty records describe this remarkable Hopi, the moral seems clear. Natives fighting to regain their independence from repressive colonial rule stand their best chance of success led by a literate, well-educated person committed to the native cause despite his familiarity with the culture of the colonial power, so that he can utilize that knowledge against it.

EFFECTS OF THE REVOLT

Hopi military strategy in the wake of the great Pueblo Revolt of 1680 significantly altered settlement patterns. Awatovi on Antelope Mesa remained where it was until its destruction. On First Mesa the Tewa-speaking refugees founded Hano, very close to where the people of Walpi constructed their post-Revolt pueblo. The latter later expanded into Sichomovi in between. The Second Mesa Hopis began building historic Shungopovi and Mishongnovi on the mesa, and later some of the Shungopovi population established Shipaulovi. Rio Grande refugees apparently built Payupki on Second Mesa. Since Oraibi on Third Mesa already occupied the mesa rim, the post–1680 movement of the other settlements left it to become the oldest continuously inhabited Hopi town. Moreover, Oraibi appears to be the longest continuously occupied North American settlement whose beginnings can be accurately dated.

By moving to the mesa rims, the Hopis transformed their society into an urban form, more cramped for living space than ever before. Each village became essentially one large apartment-house, architecturally speaking, building stone walls upward into multi-storied structures instead of spreading out. Life in these pueblos significantly influenced the development of Hopi personality, fostering a characteristic rigidity and repression of spontaneity, and generating interpersonal hostilities expressed in suspicion and accusations of witchcraft, jealousy and gossip.

While the Spanish 17th century mission effort among the Hopis must be regarded as a failure from a Roman Catholic religious point of view, economically it produced profound changes among the non-converts. Resistant as the Hopi were to Christianization, they eagerly planted the seeds of new crops introduced by the missionaries and other Spaniards, spun and wove wool from Spanish sheep, and loaded donkeys obtained from the Spaniards with firewood cut farther and farther away from the villages.

Most important of the new crops was the peach. Hopis established peach orchards at all villages wherever the trees would grow and produce fruit. Next most important in expanding Hopi diet and insuring against famine were vegetables. Watermelons, "Spanish" onions, and even the hot peppers domesticated in the New World seem to have entered Hopi cultivation during this early colonial period.

In spite of the addition of such new crops to their fields, the Hopis continued to suffer famines during historic times as a consequence of severe droughts. As early as 1659, a year of crop failure in New Mexico, Spanish records noted distribution of wheat and maize to relieve hunger at Oraibi and Shungopovi. In the 18th century, tree-ring records show that a series of drought years occurred in 1727 through 1729, in 1733, 1735, and 1737, with severe drought in 1777 that lasted through 1780. Indians reported to Governor Juan Bautista de Anza of New Mexico that hundreds of Hopis died of starvation. Reportedly, many Hopis abandoned their mesa top villages by August 1779, and sought refuge with other Indians and even exchanged their children for food, subsisting entirely on wild food during the winter, far from their comfortable homes. Thirty-three refugees migrated to Sandia. In March 1780, Friar Francisco Garcia took seventy-seven more Indians from the Hopi country to Santa Fe, and the number of reconverts reached 150 by May. Anza sent food to Tusayan Province and in September himself led yet another expedition to try again to persuade the Hopis to abandon their post-Revolt mesa-top homes for the better-watered Rio Grande Valley. Yet the Hopi, as they have always done, persevered.

Anza's 1780 expedition to Hopi country came at the end of a long series of Spanish journeys to the mesa-top, post-revolt towns to persuade New Mexico Pueblo rebels who had taken refuge among the Hopis to return to the Spanish province.

When the Hopis from other settlements destroyed Christian Awatovi, probably aided by pagan refugees from more easterly Pueblos, they actually called forth a punitive Spanish military expedition against them. New Mexico's Governor Pedro Rodriguez Cubero led his troops into Hopi country in 1701. Although the Spaniards killed and captured some Indians, the column proved unequal to the task of conquering the combined Hopi and refugee Pueblo warriors, and retreated back to the Rio Grande settlements. Governor Rodriguez Cubero's military failure to subdue the rebel Western Pueblos in 1701 set the pattern of frontier relationships for the rest of the Eighteenth Century. The effective Spanish colonial frontier remained virtually stalled not far west of Zuñi Pueblo and well to the east of the Hopi mesas

44

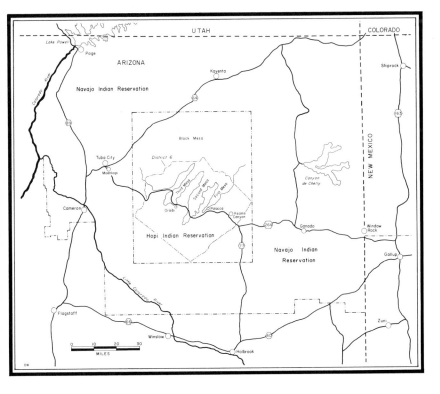

HOPI INDIAN RESERVATION, in northeastern Arizona, showing Land Use District 6 and the surrounding Navajo Indian Reservation.

from 1701 until the end of the Spanish sovereignty.

Later during the Eighteenth Century, however, Spanish missionaries and civil officials eventually achieved some success in persuading at least part of the rebel Eastern Pueblo refugees and their offspring to abandon their settlements in the Hopi country and migrate back to the Pueblos in New Mexico.

Two expeditions that Governor Francisco Cuervo Valdez sent out in 1707 apparently accomplished nothing. Governor Felix Martinez in 1716 led a large expedition as far as Walpi on First Mesa, but evidently did not attempt to storm that well-defended defensively-situated settlement. The Spaniards reported that at least one Hopi leader employed a firearm, although most Hopi warriors used bows and arrows to dissuade the Spaniards from attempting an assault up the cliff. The difficulties the Spaniards faced can be readily perceived in the aerial photograph of the First Mesa settlements taken especially for this volume which gives an eagle's eye view down the slopes the Spaniards would have had to climb to reach the Indian defenders. This Spanish expedition reportedly killed some Indians, but the troops seem to have achieved victory primarily over the maize fields that they laid waste.

In 1724 some Spanish missionaries reached the westernmost Pueblo of Oraibi, and even preached there, but without evident impact. Six years later another Franciscan traveled to Tusayan Province to preach to the Hopi and their allied Pueblo refugees, but apparently had no more success.

None of these efforts succeeded until 1742. By that time, a threat that colonial authorities might assign Hopi territory to the Jesuit Order spurred the Franciscans in New Mexico into renewed and evidently frantic efforts to prove their effectiveness either reconverting the natives of Tusayan, or at least reclaiming for Christianity and Spanish colonial rule the "apostate" New Mexico Pueblo refugee Indians still living with the Hopis. Then it was that Fathers Carlos Delgado and Ignacio de Pino persuaded a reported 441 Indians to leave the Hopi country for Sandia, Pajarito, Alameda, and other places in New Mexico from which they or their ancestors fled following the 1680 revolt. Three years later, the same energetic priests reported leading some 2,000 Indians out of Tusayan back to Isleta and Jemez. The missionaries, keeping abreast of events in the Hopi towns through native informants, sought reconverts during a period of internecine strife. The original refugees of 1680 and their descendants may well have been wearing their welcome among the Hopis rather thin by 1745, since their refuge had then lasted for up to 65 years, and they would have established rights to horticultural fields in Hopi territory only with extreme difficulty.

In 1747, Friar Miguel Menchero persuaded another group of refugees to leave Hopi territory to resettle at Sandia.

After this burst of Franciscan effort, the Tewa refugees still remained on First Mesa, where their descendants live today. The Province of Tusayan

48

LOWER VILLAGE OF MOENCOPI with terraced irrigated gardens in foreground.

continued to provide temporary refuge for other eastern Pueblo Indians seeking to escape the more burdensome features of colonial rule. Yet the total population of the Hopi country had undoubtedly been significantly reduced by Spanish resettlement of former refugee eastern Pueblos, diminishing human pressure on horticultural and wild food resources. On the other hand, the departure of refugees left appreciably fewer warriors to defend the Hopi towns against Navajo and other raiders.

Apparently not for another quarter century did Franciscan priests again visit the Hopis and Hopi–Tewas, and then the visitors were of quite a different type. Both were renowned explorers who understood Indians well enough to journey hundreds of miles through unknown tribes and return in one piece. In 1775, Friar Silvestre Velez de Escalante passed through Hano, the Hopi–Tewa village, Walpi, Mishongnovi, Shipaulovi, Shungopavi, and Oraibi during an eight-day reconnaissance, upon returning from an exploration far into the unknown lands of the Utes and Paiutes to the northwest. Escalante noted in his diary that:

"The Moqui [the Spanish name for Hopi] are very civilized, apply themselves to weaving and cultivating the land by means of which they raise abundant crops of maize, beans and chile. They also gather cotton, although not much. They suffer from scarcity of wood and good water . . . but owned flocks of sheep, some cattle, and good horse herds."

The following year, that of America's independence, Friar Francisco Garces, missionary at San Xavier del Bac on the Sonoran frontier, reached the Hopis. Following Havasupai guides over the trade route from the lower Colorado River, Garces entered the westernmost Hopi settlement of Oraibi on July 2.

The Hopis received Garces coldly. Garces himself surmised this occurred because he came from Northern Piman territory, and the Hopis remembered their early historic military falling out with their former trading friends. On July 4, Garces turned back. Four years later, the Hopis admitted to Governor Anza, an old friend of Garces when both served in Sonora, that they feared that their discourtesy to Garces had something to do with causing the drought that began the year following his visit. On the trail back to Sonora, Garces noted that Hopi blankets traveled far along the inter-tribal trade routes he followed.

A quarter-century earlier, a Jesuit missionary already reported that Hopi textiles reached the Piman-speaking Indians inhabiting the Gila River frontier of Sonora, via the lower Colorado River Halchid-homas. The Hopis probably traded their textiles to Northeastern Pai Indians for buckskins, dried *Agave* pulp or red ochre, and the latter passed the blankets on to the Halchidhomas on the Colorado who bartered them to the Gila River peoples. The Jesuit record suggests that Hopi blankets constituted something of a definite standard of value to other tribes, if not precisely a true medium of exchange.

The Spanish documents record the importance of Hopi textiles, from the offer of 600 pieces of woven goods to the Espejo contingent in 1583 to the Jesuit–Franciscan record of inter-tribal trade in Hopi textiles in 1746–1776. This record may reflect a continuation of prehistoric importance of Hopi cotton textiles, or an increasing importance of cotton and later woolen textile production during the historic period. In either case, the record clearly shows that textile export earned vital "foreign exchange" credits for the Hopis that enabled them to augment their own food production, and import ceremonial pigments and other items during a 200-year period of time.

MEXICAN RULE

Spanish dominion over the Hopi ended in 1821 when Mexico gained its independence. The Mexicans were too busy with internal problems farther south to pay much attention to these northern pueblos. No missionaries were sent, nor aid offered during the brief period of Mexican sovereignty.

In fact, the Mexican Province of New Mexico proved unequal to the task of excluding Anglo–American mountain men from Mexican territory. In 1834, for example, a small party of pelt seekers atttempted to raid some Hopi gardens. They were repulsed only after the loss of some fifteen to twenty Hopi lives.

The Navajo, whose expanding population began migrating close to the Hopi defensive villages in late Spanish colonial times, continued to harass the Hopis during the Mexican period. Just as the weak Mexican frontier forces could not keep U. S. citizens out of their territory, they proved unequal to the military task of curbing Navajo economic raiding of the Hopi, New Mexico Pueblos, and the Mexican settlements as well.

The Mexican sovereignty ended with the conquest of the area by United States forces during the Mexican War in 1846–48. With Navajos making Hopi life unsafe, these Indians understandably looked to the new sovereign power for military aid. Indeed, a group of Hopis traveled to Santa Fe in 1850, two years after the American conquest, to see James Calhoun, the first U. S. Indian Agent for the Territory of New Mexico. They wanted to ascertain the "purposes and views of the government of the United States toward them." They also complained "bitterly of the depredations of the Navajos." It was not until 1863 that these depredations were halted when American forces, under the command of Colonel Kit Carson finally subdued the major Navajo warrior groups in Canyon de Chelly near Fort Defiance.

This, however, did not put an end to searing drought, nor to the scourge of smallpox. The Hopi were besieged by both, in 1853 and 1854, and again a decade later. From 1853 to 1861, the Hopi population decreased an estimated 60 per cent.

With the coming of Anglo–Americans, new attempts to convert the Hopi to Christianity began. The Mormon leader Brigham Young ordered the noted "Apostle to the Lamanites," Jacob Hamblin,

54

to the Hopis in the fall of 1858. At Oraibi, Hamblin's party met a chief known as "Tuba" who escorted the missionaries to the other Hopi pueblos. Speculating that the Hopis might speak a Welch dialect, Hamblin took both a Spanish and a Welch interpreter. The latter proved of absolutely no use. Hamblin did encounter Hopis with whom he could converse in Ute, and saw Navajos freely enter Hopi pueblos to watch the preaching.

The arrival of Mormon missionaries set off a grave debate among Hopi leaders on the question whether Hamblin and his companions were the prophets Hopi tradition predicted would appear to lead them. A negative decision by the Indians, coupled with what the modern social scientist recognizes as cultural shock, led the Mormons to withdraw in November of 1859. Hamblin conducted three missionaries to the Hopis late in 1862. He then took three Hopi men back to Salt Lake City despite their fears of crossing the Colorado River. Hamblin returned these visitors to their homes in April of 1863 and evacuated his missionaries. He visited the Hopis again in 1865 to try to persuade them to move to Utah and settle among the Mormons, but they refused. The Hopis gave Hamblin a cool reception when he returned in 1869 leading twenty Whites and twenty Paiutes. Thus, even though Hamblin entered the Hopi mission field a dozen years in advance of other Anglo–Americans, the Church of Latter Day Saints failed to win any Hopi converts prior to 1870, when traders and

Protestant missionaries arrived and built a mission school at Keams Canyon, a dozen miles east of First Mesa.

Once again, missionaries brought the Hopis new crops which these Indians rapidly incorporated into their horticulture, whatever the failure of the religious conversion efforts. The Hopi term for turban squash, "Mormon pumpkin," indicates that these Indians obtained this food plant from the early Mormon missionaries at the mesas or at Moencopi. Not until Hopis moved out to colonize Moencopi, with its springs allowing irrigation, did they begin to grow wheat regularly, the Spanish missionaries having failed to introduce this as a permanent crop some two centuries earlier. Mormon farmers also probably introduced the safflower and sorghum to Hopi farmers.

Though relatively conservative in their religious beliefs, the Hopis demonstrated considerable flexibility in horticultural practices. They selected new crops and fiber and meat-producing livestock enthusiastically, undoubtedly enhancing their ability to survive in an environment that can only be characterized as marginal for sedentary agriculturists.

ESTABLISHMENT OF THE RESERVATION

In 1869, the United States government appointed a special Indian agent just for the Hopis and, in 1882, the Hopi Indian Reservation of 3,863 square miles was established by executive order. A government school was built at the agency at Keams Canyon in the year 1887.

Protestant missionaries, representing a number of denominations, moved into the Hopi country during this period. In 1870, the Moravians established a mission at Oraibi. Five years later, the Baptists built one on Second Mesa. In 1893, the Mennonite missionary, H. R. Voth, settled at Oraibi. A paradox, Voth simultaneously attempted to stamp out native religious beliefs and to preserve them in well-done ethnographic reports prepared for the Field Museum of Natural History in Chicago.

The agents of the federal government were no less zealous in their efforts to turn the Hopis into conformists who would behave as they thought good Whites should. Attendance at the Keams Canyon school was compulsory, although many Hopis refused to send their children. Hopis were supposed to look like White people, and one agent, shortly after the turn of the century, had Hopis tied with barbed wire while their hair was cut. Censuses were taken, but were incomplete because some of the Indians, notably those from Oraibi, refused to cooperate. The Bureau of Indian Affairs, acting through the Land Allotment Act of 1887, attempted to individualize clan-held lands; Hopis surreptitiously removed the surveyors' stakes. Federal troops were sent to discipline Hopi leaders and, while the Indians resisted, some were imprisoned at Alcatraz for "seditious acts." Hopis, especially at Oraibi, gained a reputation for being hostile and recalcitrant. Meanwhile, more government schools were established, at Oraibi and below First Mesa.

In spite of this turmoil and forceful imposition of Anglo–American legal standards on the Hopi, some of them preferred the White man's ways. They wanted their children to be educated in the government schools; they listened to the fundamentalist missionaries. And so, existing Hopi factionalism was exacerbated by social schism along religious lines. This precipitated a volatile factionalism among the Hopi, an internal strife that reached a breaking point at Oraibi in the fall of 1906.

The traditional element, termed "Hostiles" as opposed to the progressives, called "Friendlies" by the Whites, clashed not only over relationships with the federal government, but also over native religious calendars. The strife was at first verbal but soon became a pushing, shoving melee on the outskirts of the village. The conservative leader, perhaps in an effort to avoid bloodshed, did exactly what Hopis at Kawaiokuh did with the Spaniards more than four hundred years earlier. He drew a line in the sand. He turned to the progressive leader and said: "If your men are strong enough to push us away from the village to pass me over the line, it will be done." With his own people pushing and the opposing side shoving him back, the traditionalist leader was severely mauled. Finally, he was moved far back from the line, and the traditionalists agreed to move from the village. Near the scene is a commemorative of the event marked in the sandstone bedrock. It shows

Courtesy of Southwest Museum

A RARE PHOTOGRAPH of Hopi men imprisoned at Alcatraz for "seditious acts" against the United States following the General Allotment Act of 1887.

the line and the clan symbols of the opposing leaders. The inscription reads: "Well it have to be this way now that when you pass me over this line it will be DONE." The date was September 8, 1906.

Thus, for the first time since the later Spanish period, Hopi villages were split asunder. The conservatives, packing whatever they could on their backs, moved out that very afternoon, and camped at Hotevilla, several miles to the west on Third Mesa. Shortly thereafter, U. S. troops arrived and imprisoned leaders on both sides and many of the "Hostile" able-bodied men, leaving women, children, and the aged to eke out an existence at the new settlement with a cold winter coming on. Thus did federal authorities continue to foster cultural atomism among the Hopi.

When some less conservative Hotevillans tried to return to Oraibi but were rejected, they founded in 1907 another new village called Bakabi. Then, after one of the imprisoned leaders returned in 1910 to decree that no Christian convert could live at Oraibi, other Hopis formed Kyakotsmovi ("New Oraibi") below the mesa.

In the ensuing decades another type of conflict began to arise between Hopis and migrant Navajos who by then had completely surrounded the Hopi Reservation. While Hopi need for grazing land increased, so did the Navajo population and its flocks of sheep. A number of boundary conflicts occurred between individuals of the two tribes. By the bebeginning of World War II, Navajos inhabited and

61

grazed their flocks over almost three-quarters of the 1882 Hopi Reservation. The Bureau of Indian Affairs, reading the letter of the original executive order, which said that the Hopi Reservation had been established for Hopis "and other Indians," ruled in favor of the Navajos. The one-fourth residue remaining to the Hopi was designated as Land Use District Six. Grazing held great economic importance for the Hopis themselves by that time, since livestock brought in 34 per cent of the nearly $280,000 total Hopi income in 1942.

The federal government also intervened in Hopi life in other ways. In 1935, one year after Congress passed the Wheeler–Howard (or Indian Reorganization) Act, the Bureau of Indian Affairs urged the Hopi to become an organized "tribe" in the Anglo–American sense of the word. The Hopi adopted a constitution and bylaws in 1936 establishing nine voting districts. The Tewas and Hopis living on First Mesa agreed to work together, so had four delegates on the Tribal Council. On Second Mesa, Mishongnovi elected two, Shipaulovi, one and Shungopovi, two delegates. At Third Mesa, Oraibi chose one, New Oraibi, two, Hotevilla, two and Bakabi, one delegate. Moencopi chose two councilmen.

The Tribal Council met for the first time in 1937, its members mostly drawn from the continuing progressive ranks. Again, Oraibi, among other villages, refused to recognize this new "democracy by fiat." Historically, each Hopi village was autonomous and the people possessed little or no sense of tribal unity, even though residents of all settlements spoke a common language after the departure of the last Rio Grande Pueblo refugees in the mid–18th century. (The Tewas of Hano became bilingual in their own language and Hopi.) Meeting only sporadically, the all-Hopi Council achieved little initial success. A law and order code adopted in 1940 is now enforced by a Tribal Court with judge, assistant and necessary policemen.

By the time of the second World War, the Hopi way of life had changed greatly under the influence of industrial technology. These Indians employed manufactured farming implements and household utensils, wore mostly manufactured clothing — cheap cotton prints for the women and velveteen blouses with blue jeans or white twill for the men — and consumed numerous processed foods imported to the mesas. So great had Hopi dependence upon food and manufactured imports from wider United States society become, as a matter of fact, that no less than sixteen traders dealt with them. Goods moved over vehicular roads constructed to the mesas, and the Hopis themselves drove over those roads in horse-drawn wagons and even a few automobiles.

Wage labor already brought the Hopis 36 per cent of the total 1942 income, compared to only 2 per cent from arts and crafts and 22 per cent from agriculture. Hopi wage income has steadily increased in absolute value and proportion of total income since that time. United States coins and currency have circulated more and more abundantly among the Hopi, who in

63

recent years have opened bank accounts in Winslow, Holbrook, Flagstaff, and even Phoenix.

Following World War II, factionalism between "conservative" and "progressive" Hopis continued. At issue were the building of new schools and paved roads, and drilling of water wells and oil wells, and many other matters. In fact, almost anything proposed by the Bureau of Indian Affairs or the Tribal Council was opposed by the traditionalist leaders centered primarily at Hotevilla and Shungopovi. In 1953, when the all-Hopi Tribal Council became the *official* governing body of the Hopi Tribe, most Hopis thought of it as a "rubber stamp" for the actions of the Bureau. Traditionalist spokesmen sought to enlist such Anglo–American organizations as the New Mexico Association on Indian Affairs and the Arizona Council for Civic Unity in their opposition to the Bureau and Tribal Council, making effective use of newspaper reporters to generate favorable public sentiment.

Somewhat paradoxically, traditionalist opposition to Bureau and Council actions extended even to Hopi attempts to obtain legally the return of lands within the original 1882 executive order Reservation.

An act of the United States Congress in 1958, stemming from a bill introduced by Arizona's Senator Barry Goldwater, set up a three-man special court to hear the dispute. In a judgment handed down by that court in 1962, these judges gave the Hopis exclusive use of 600,000 acres of the 1882 Reservation, exclusive of District Six. In addition, the court established Hopi interest in one million additional acres of land.

This factionalism, dividing "traditional" and "progressive" Hopi elements, and indeed, to one extent or another, all Hopis, continues to this day.

So it has been that the Hopi and their culture have existed on their northern Arizona mesas for at least 1,500 years. The last four centuries, from the time of first European contact, have been marked by torture, conflict, frustration, and deceit, and administration of Hopi affairs, marked by a high degree of ethnocentrism on the part of the Whites. Other peoples have culturally buckled under much less. Yet the Hopi, who have been in contact with Whites longer than any other tribe in Arizona, in spite of these seemingly insurmountable obstacles, continue to maintain one of the most traditional Indian cultures in the United States. It is in their cultural patterns and values that an understanding of this seeming paradox must be sought.

Most Hopi villages sit today just where they were built subsequent to the Pueblo Revolt of 1680. Only Oraibi, probably founded about A.D. 1300, is older. Since the turn of the century, two other towns have grown up in the valleys below Second Mesa and First Mesa; these are Toreva and Polacca respectively. Moencopi, now divided into upper (progressive) and lower (conservative) segments, some forty miles west of Oraibi, originally began as a farming colony from that mother village; it still owes a degree of loyalty to Oraibi. Finally, there is the Tewa-speaking village dating from 1680 on First Mesa.

The finger-like mesas upon which most of the Hopi villages are located are mostly exposed bedrock of Mesa Verde sandstone. Shallow deposits of windblown sand provide bare anchorage for grass, stunted juniper trees and occasionally peach trees that the Hopi acquired from the Spaniards.

The valleys below are deep with water-laid alluvium. They are dissected by deep arroyos, incised after 1880. These, from west to east, are the Dinnebito, Oraibi, Wepo, and Polacca "washes." They carry water only in the spring runoff or after heavy summer cloudbursts. Their waters are too ephemeral and too deeply entrenched to be used for irrigation; in fact, only at Moencopi and Hotevilla are there small, spring-fed irrigation systems.

In the American Southwest, precipitation is generally directly proportionate and temperature indirectly proportionate to altitude. The average elevation of the Hopi mesas is 6,500 feet. Precipitation, in the form of winter snows and mid-summer rains varies from 10 inches annually in the lower reaches to 13 inches on the higher mesas. The mean annual temperature, as recorded at the Keams Canyon agency, is 51° F. While, at this latitude and elevation there are four distinct seasons, two characteristics of the climate remain the same. There is a relatively small amount of cloudiness and an abundance of clear weather. Secondly, there is a daily temperature variation, averaging from night to day about 30 de-

HOPI MAIDEN, photographed at Oraibi about 1890, cooking in pueblo style corner fireplace. The corn mush is being cooked in a native pot. Corn meal is in the basket at right foreground and a yucca whisk broom lies on the firewood.

grees. The frost-free growing season is between 150 and 120 days, except at Moencopi where it is between 180 and 150 days. Aside from recent arroyo cutting, the environment of the Hopi country has not changed greatly since it was first settled by the Anasazi ancestors of these Pueblo farmers.

Obviously, the Hopi country is too dry for the people to depend upon rainfall alone for the maturation of their crops. While special, drought-resistant varieties of corn have been developed, the Hopi also take excellent advantage of micro-environmental niches. They have developed at least four different farming techniques. Flood-water farming in areas where floods from small drainages spread in thin sheets of water over the crops is most important. Planting in sand dunes is another widespread practice. To the unaccustomed eye, this seems to border on the incredible. Yet the Hopi learned long ago that the sand acts as a dry mulch. Even in the driest season of the year one can dig down a few inches in the sand and find moisture. Hopis plant some fields often only a few square yards in extent, where seepage from the rocks will provide some amounts of water. Here they grow a few crops, especially at Moencopi and Hotevilla, on terraces irrigated from small springs. Hopi horticulturists usually reserve these terraces for less common garden crops such as chiles, onions, and similar domestic plants. They also grow some peaches, the stunted trees usually located in the sand dunes. Altogether, the Hopis cultivate some forty domesticated plants plus another ten semi-domesticated ones, such as devil's claw (*Martynia*), beeweed beebalm (a wild mint), tobacco, dock, potato, cat-tail, and willow and cottonwood trees.

Sheep raising formerly was of more importance to the Hopi than it is today. Edicts from the Bureau of Indian Affairs have required Hopis to pasture and corral their sheep far from the villages, so that it is no longer feasible, from a time point of view, to herd large flocks.

Wild plants still assume a major place in Hopi economy. Almost half of the plants that grow in their country have some practical use, either as food, in manufactures, or for ceremonial purposes. In fact, Hopis frequently make the long 80-mile trip to the San Francisco Peaks near Flagstaff for ceremonial plants such as tobacco, white and Douglas fir, and aspen, as well as pine logs for roof beams, mountain mahogany for dyeing leather, oak and holly, grape-wood for weapons and tool-making, and beebalm to use as a food seasoning.

In sum, the Hopis are environmental wizards, having a very practical knowledge of the natural world about them. They do not take advantage of it but attempt to follow an explicit philosophy of working harmoniously within it.

DEVELOPMENT OF HOPI CRAFTS

In recent years the Hopi economic base has broadened somewhat. Always excellent craftsmen and artists, their craft outlets have increased. This is in

70

part due to efforts on the part of anthropologists at the Museum of Northern Arizona in Flagstaff who, as early as the 1930s, encouraged Hopis to produce fine, native-style articles of all types. As an inducement, the Museum established an annual Hopi Craftsman exhibit, held around the fourth of July. The items exhibited are the finest that the Hopi produce and are offered for sale to the thousands of visitors who attend the exhibit, all proceeds being returned to the individual Hopi craftsman. In addition, a Hopi Tribal Arts and Crafts Guild flourishes, with a large sales shop located next to the new and startlingly designed Tribal Museum and Cultural Center on Second Mesa. Several individually owned shops also are flourishing.

Hopi crafts are varied and authentic. On Third Mesa women make beautiful and useful wicker baskets decorated with native dyes and yucca "sifter" baskets similar to those produced by their ancestors as early as A.D. 500. On Second Mesa the basketry woven is of the coiled variety, quite distinct from that made on Third Mesa. First Mesa is the locus of virtually all pottery manufacture, and women of the Tewa village as well as of the two Hopi communities produce large quantities of finely made polychrome and black-on-yellow vessels of many traditional forms. While the ceramic art deteriorated badly in the late 19th century on all three mesas, it was only on First Mesa that a revival was attempted.

Before the turn of the century, the Smithsonian Institution archaeologist, Jesse Walter Fewkes, was excavating in the ruins of Sikyatki, below First Mesa. This village had been occupied about A.D. 1300 until shortly after the Spaniards arrived, a period of great florescence in the polychrome and yellow-ware period of the art. Fewkes employed many Hopi and Tewa workmen, one of whom frequently took fragments of this finely designed pottery home to his wife, Nampeyo. She became intrigued with the old shapes and designs and began reproducing them in her own vessels, a tradition that continues to be carried on by her Tewa granddaughters.

Men on all three mesas engage in other crafts, especially weaving and the carving of kachina dolls, small representations of Hopi supernaturals. Throughout recorded history, the men have been the weavers, and they produce blankets and most ceremonial costumes such as kilts, shawls, sashes, and leggings. The religious garments are not only made for their own use but also for trade with the New Mexico pueblos, where the art of weaving has disappeared.

LIVING PATTERNS IN TRANSITION

No longer, however, do most Hopis, except possibly the very old and ultra-conservative, wear native clothing. In times past, women wore a hand woven, indigo *manta,* a loosely fitting, off the shoulder garment that reached from the shoulder to just below the knees and was belted at the waist. Unmarried girls wore their hair in a highly distinctive "butterfly whorl," while married women effected two simple "braids" at the side of the head.

Men traditionally wore a loose cotton shirt and trousers, slit on the sides to the knee, and moccasins. In warm weather sometimes only a breechcloth was used, while in the winter a warm and serviceable rabbit fur robe was worn. Men's hair was usually banged in front and tied in a queue in the back. A colored headband was folded and tied over the forehead.

Today, most women wear cotton house dresses and brightly colored shawls, while men have taken over more typical Anglo western dress of cotton shirt and Levis. Hopis rarely wear hats.

Hopi architecture has, with the exception of the addition of doors and window glass, changed little from late prehistoric times. Houses, usually contiguous and sometimes two stories in height, are of sandstone masonry with mud mortar. Inside, one usually finds two or possibly three rooms, the walls neatly plastered in white. One room would serve as a kitchen-dining room; another, a living-bedroom; while the third usually functions as a storeroom. The ceilings are in a typical pueblo tradition, spanned with large, peeled pine timbers or *vigas*. At right angles to these are smaller poles or shakes. In older houses, masses of cliff rose branches are used. The whole is then covered with mud, sloped on the exterior to provide drainage to *canales* leading off the roof.

Until the period of World War II, very little

furniture would have been found in Hopi houses. People slept on sheepskins and ate their meals from common bowls on the floor. Since that time, however, Hopis have furnished their houses with tables, chairs, beds, dressers, and wood- and coal-burning cooking stoves.

Even more recently, there has been a trend toward the construction of cinder block or concrete block buildings, usually separated by some distance from the main village buildings.

Other types of structures also mark the typical Hopi town. Each village has several subterranean, rectangular *kivas*, entered usually by means of a ladder protruding from a hole in the roof, or less frequently, by a side entrance accessible from a steeply sloping ramp leading from the surface of the ground. The *kivas* are about 27 feet long, 13 feet wide, and 7 feet high. They are, in effect, "divided" into two portions: toward the rear is a slightly smaller, raised area where women sit during non-secret ceremonies; the main floor, surrounded by a low seating bench on three sides, is the actual dance area during religious performances. When such rites are not being observed in the *kivas*, they serve as men's "clubhouses" where the members of the *kiva* group come to talk, smoke, and, at least in former times, carry on weaving activities.

Tucked away in the villages near the houses are very small masonry rooms containing a corner fire area. This small section of the room is covered by a smooth, flat, rectangular stone, under which a fire

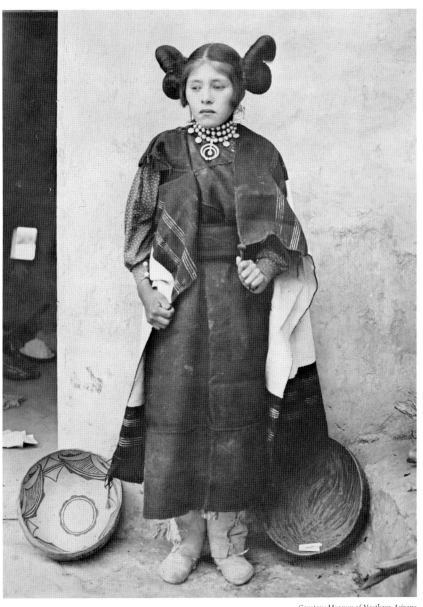

HOPI MAIDEN in handwoven dress and shawl, handmade buckskin boots, Navajo silver necklace. She stands between two Hopi ceramic bowls. Photograph probably taken around the turn of the century.

is built. These are *piki* houses, where women cook the delicious wafer-like corn bread that is used on all feast day occasions.

Outlying from the villages are similarly small, one-room structures that are called peach houses. During the peach harvest, women use these for shelter and storage while they are drying their peaches on the warm sandstone ledges just below the crests of the mesas.

Today, even the casual visitor to the Hopi towns notices rather large-scale adoptions of Anglo–American materials and goods. In addition to the architectural aspects and items of household furniture already mentioned, some of the villages (all save the most conservative) have commercial electric power. While the garish power poles and lines seem incongruously set in the ages-old villages, the electricity they furnish does provide some modern conveniences. One elderly woman on First Mesa said of the electricity: "As for me, I don't need it, but it is certainly nice to have good light for the children to do their homework by."

While many Hopis are still good runners — they furnished at least one long-distance Olympic champion in the early days of this century — and most think nothing of walking several miles to their corn fields, the pickup truck has become ubiquitous. Since there is one paved highway dissecting the Hopi Reservation now, families use these trucks to journey to Keams Canyon, to the Agency, or to the Public Health Service Hospital, or to "border" towns such as Holbrook, Winslow, or Flagstaff for shopping expeditions.

Bureau of Indian Affairs day schools are in operation near all three mesas. These take Hopi students only through the eighth grade and there is no high school on the Reservation. Therefore, Hopis wishing to continue their education must leave home during this crucial maturation period and go to boarding schools such as the Phoenix Indian School. Until the 1940s, the day schools were located in close proximity to the villages, although below them, so that children could easily scamper up and down to and from school. Parents could easily make visits also and so talk with teachers about their children's affairs. More recently, modern educational plants and teachers' quarters have been constructed, quite in disharmony with native architecture, some distances in the valleys below the mesas. Children are bussed to and from their homes. No longer is there the close rapport between school and home. As one Anglo teacher said when asked how she liked teaching in the Hopi country: "Oh, it's all right, except that there are no people here." People to her were Whites, her own kind. Further inquiry revealed that in three years of teaching Hopi children she had never visited their homes.

SOCIAL, RELIGIOUS, POLITICAL STRUCTURE

Of all existing Hopi cultural institutions, those that are most important and those from which most of their deeply held values spring, are their religion, their social structure, and their political organization. While Hopis have adopted many items of Anglo material goods, it is in the non-material sphere of their lives that traditional patterns have remained to give most Hopis a strong sense of security in their otherwise troubled world. Most of these socio-political and religious patterns have changed very little since aboriginal times.

The basic unit in Hopi society is the extended family. There is a mother-father-children relationship grown larger through the pattern of husbands moving to their wives' homes in this society which reckons descent through the female line. A typical Hopi household, then, consists of the simple family, the wife's parents, her unmarried brothers, her sisters and their husbands, and children. While the Hopi are monogamous, their unions have been characterized as being very "brittle" and divorce is frequent. At the dissolution of a marriage, the husband usually returns to his maternal home with which he has always maintained his closest ties. The importance of the women in a Hopi family cannot be overestimated. They dominate all activities and it is the wise man who maintains the support of the females in his household. The behavior of a woman's sisters toward her children is essentially similar to that of the mother herself. Indeed, Hopi children acknowledge this relationship by calling their biological mother and her sisters all by the same kinship term for mother. At the same time, while a father's relations to his children, especially boys, is very close, they nevertheless belong to their mother's clan. In this social context, the father has very little to do with the disciplining of his offspring. This is left to the mother's brother, of the same clan as his sister's children, a phenomenon very common in matrilineal societies (those which reckon descent through women).

Hopi clans, consisting of all the known or presumed descendants of a common ancestress, also perform important functions in the society. There are 21 matrilineal clans, each with a head woman, usually the oldest female in the clan. Clan members marry members of other clans, marriage between clan members being prohibited. The clans, or more specifically, the lineages within them, are said to "own" the agricultural lands which are distributed among members so long as the latter make use of them. More importantly, Hopi clans are involved in the very complicated religious ceremonies of the villages. Clans "own" or control the major ceremonies; these ceremonies are performed by members of secret religious societies; the head of each society is ideally the brother of the head woman of the clan.

There is much more to Hopi religion than that. For religion, to the traditional Hopi, is a core about which life evolves. So, it is a great motivating influence in the everyday lives of the people. Indeed, it would not be overstating the case to say that the Hopi are among the most thoroughly religious people in the world.

Hopi religion is based upon certain primary prin-

Photograph by John Griffin

PORTION OF SHUNGOPOVI showing the older, two story houses and a modern home on the right.

ciples that include: a belief in the continuity of life after death; that Nature and God are one; unchangeableness — the absolute reliability of the universe and nature; and the presence of a spirit-being in every object — clouds, rain, animals, birds, plants, rocks, and mountains. These spirits, furthermore, can be appeased, made friendly, and thus caused to intercede before the gods in behalf of the Hopi.

The Hopi pantheon holds seven principal deities: the creator of the earth; the guardian of life; the creator of life; a great serpent form that controls life blood, vegetal sap, and especially water; death or the destroyer; the deity of rain clouds; and the sun. Religious ceremonies are performed throughout the year to these seven deities as well as to many others of lesser importance.

The Hopi do not, however, pray directly to these gods. Rather, appeals and acknowledgments of gratitude are sent to the gods through designated associated animistic spirits or *kachinas*. All Hopis, both males and females, are initiated into the *kachina* cult, nowadays at the age of seven or eight. Only males can portray the masked impersonators of these super-naturals. There are about 30 primary *kachinas* who take part in five major ceremonies, but there are several hundred *kachinas* of lesser importance also. The Hopi believe that these *kachinas*, for the most part, have their homes in the San Francisco Peaks near Flagstaff. From late in December until mid-July of each year, they come to the villages to help the people, especially in their quest for rain and for good crops. Putting it another way, *kachinas* are thought of as generalized ancestors who return with clouds and rain to help the community. They normally come in groups to dance in the *kivas* or in the plazas. After the important Winter Solstice or Soyal ceremony, during which the *kachinas* make their first appearance of the ceremonial year, *kachina* dances are held frequently throughout the spring and early summer. While any well-behaved man in a village may request the Village "Chief's" permission to sponsor a *kachina* performance, the dances themselves are performed by male members of particular *kivas*. The occasion, whether during the cold early spring nights in the *kivas* or during warm summer days in the plazas, is filled with excitement and activity. The dance is usually very formal, serious, and rhythmical. At the same time, however, at the plaza dances, the seriousness is relieved by the antics of clown or Mudhead *kachinas*. These representations, always separated from the main lines of dancers, carry on all sorts of impromptu humorous activities, frequently at the expense of the spectators, especially Whites. The last *kachina* performance in mid-July is the Niman or Homegoing dance, after which the *kachinas* are thought to return to their mythical mountain home until the following December.

In addition to Hopi *kachina* ceremonies, there are a number of important secret religious societies concerned with rain, curing, clowning, and, in the past, war. While the ceremonies performed by these societies are thought to be owned by particular clans that also furnish the head priest of the society, membership in any particular society cuts across the whole clan system. A Hopi may join a society in a number of ways, but all involve long and complicated initiation rites. A young man, after being initiated into the *kachina* cult, normally undergoes induction in what may be loosely termed a "tribal initiation" which is performed periodically by four men's societies. While this rite is very complex and not fully understood by outsiders, it dramatizes the emergence of the Hopi from their mythical "underworld" and prepares the initiates for their ultimate position in that "underworld" after death. Two of these societies are in general concerned with fertility, while the other two have a more warlike character.

Initiation into one of the four divisions of the "tribal initiation" ceremony is a prerequisite for participation in the Soyal, or great Winter Solstice ceremony which is the keystone of the Hopi ceremonial system. Other societies are associated with rain and curing and have a more restricted membership and a lesser role in the ceremonial cycle. For example, the Blue Flute and the Gray Flute societies perform a joint ceremony on alternate years to produce rain for maturing crops. The Snake and the Antelope societies likewise perform a joint ceremony, alternating with those of the Flute societies. The last day public performance of the Snake–Antelope rites is the most widely publicized ceremony of the Hopis. The rites serve a number of complex functions. They are associated with rain making, with sun worship, with plant germination, growth, and maturity, with death, and, again in former times, with war. The snakes themselves are thought of as messengers to be released after the long ritual.

Three exclusively women's societies, patterned after those of the men, have functions similar to the others.

The very complicated religion of the Hopi can be understood only with respect to other aspects of their culture. For at least a thousand years they and their ancestors have lived in an arid region, relying primarily upon agriculture as a food source. They have always lived in more or less compact villages where the introduction of contagious disease has had a terrifying consequence for the population. The Hopi were never completely free from raids by more warlike people. Since their material resources for offsetting these dangers and anxieties were scanty, they resorted to supernatural means to give them assurance that they would not be destroyed. As one outstanding student of the Hopi, Mischa Titiev, has said: "Against each of the perils which endangered Hopi society their ceremonial system opposed a comforting buffer. . . . Shorn of its elaborate, detailed and colorful superstructure of costumes, songs and dances, the entire complex of Hopi religious behavior stands revealed as a unified attempt to safeguard Hopi society from the danger of disintegration and dissolution." Indeed, without their native religion it can safely be said that Hopis would not have been able to survive centuries of adversity.

HOPI SNAKE DANCE at the Second Mesa pueblo of Mishongnovi, August, 1907. These are the summer rites of the Snake–Antelope society photographed before the Hopi prohibited the taking of pictures of their religious observances. The snake dance, functioning primarily in weather control, is held in any one village every other year, alternating with the ceremony of the Blue Flute society. The bower of cottonwood branches to the left is the *kisi*, where the snakes are kept.

Not only is Hopi social structure inextricably interwoven with religion, but their political organization is similarly tied. Leaving aside for the moment the official Tribal Council, each Hopi village is an autonomous political unit, a functioning theocracy. The head priests of the several societies of each village lead its government. The priest of the most important society is thought of as the "village chief."

The imposition by the United States government of "democracy" to supplant "theocracy" has been one of the great causes of friction among Hopis in recent years. The traditionalists or conservatives have, by and large, refused to recognize the Council, while the more progressive Hopis usually take a diametrically opposing view.

While Hopi social structure and religion continue to assume a very vital role in the lives of most Hopis — indeed, there is a resurgence of native religious fervor in some villages — the two opposing political systems continue to cause conflict.

THE FUTURE

Difficult as prognostication is, the thousand-year-long record of Hopi cultural development outlined here allows certain predictions about the Hopi future to be made with considerable confidence.

Biological Survival

The first prediction that can be made is that the Hopi Indians will survive into the foreseeable future as a biologically distinct ethnic group. The intransigent "Hopiness" of the culturally conservative

Hopis makes them reluctant to mate with non-Hopis, and will continue to do so in the future. At the same time, even conservative Hopis have learned something about principles of household and personal hygiene, and public health policies in the United States have gone far toward eradicating smallpox and other contagious diseases that once decimated the Hopis. Public Health Service measures to effect sanitary domestic water supplies and the existence of a modern hospital at the Keams Canyon agency have cut the abnormally large infantile mortality rate. Thus, Hopi population seems assured biologically for a long time to come.

This is not to say that Hopis will not intermingle with members of other ethnic groups. They have, do, and will surely do so in the future. Numerous Hopis have married Indians of other tribes, including the very Navajos who have competed with the Hopis for scarce resources within the 1882 Reservation boundaries. The culturally "progressive" Hopis and even some conservatives can be expected to continue this pattern of admixture with other Indians, to produce a less parochial, more generalized "Indian" minority in the United States population.

Ethnic exogamy does not always involve other Indians living in the historic Hopi settlements. Quite often it involves Hopis moving away to live in other Reservation communities, or in ethnically mixed towns, even abandoning the female descent principle. The future will almost surely bring a greater geographic dispersion of persons who are

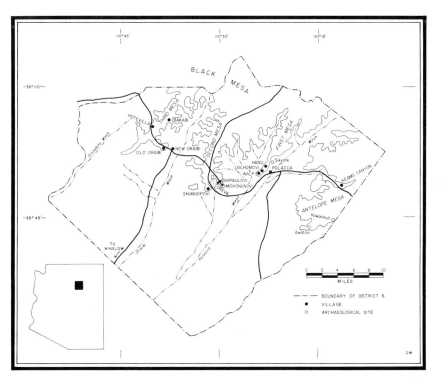

LAND USE DISTRICT 6, approximately one-fourth of the Executive Order Hopi Reservation.

biologically Hopi but who culturally participate in wider United States society. Many Hopis already have migrated away from the ancestral villages at the south edge of Black Mesa to live in railroad towns such as Holbrook and Winslow and Flagstaff, and even major metropolitan areas such as Phoenix. More Hopis are likely to migrate to these places as individuals learn the skills in demand in industrial society.

Factionalism

Implicit in our forecast for the patterns of Hopi biological survival is the expectation that Hopi social factions will not only endure, but become even more important than at present. What we anticipate will happen sociologically among Hopi individuals is a widening dichotomy between the "traditional" or "conservative" Hopis and those who find other religious systems and economic pursuits more congenial than the traditional ones. It is the latter individuals we expect to emigrate away from the historic Hopi settlements to the ethnically mixed towns and cities. It is the former we expect to remain in the historic towns and attempt to pursue the ancient patterns of economic activity and the accustomed routines of religious ritual.

We anticipate that Hopis will continue to diverge culturally, with one group stubbornly trying to maintain a traditional way of life in the historic towns and another moving into ethnically mixed settlements to follow a life-style very like that of Whites, Blacks, and others. Nevertheless, we perceive certain dynamic influences tempering the present extremism in leadership of the so-called "traditional Hopi chiefs." The nearly automatic negative response to external initiatives has already more than once placed the extremist leadership in a locally untenable position. One example is the extremist leadership's opposition to Hopi participation in legal actions aimed toward establishing Hopi control over the lands within the 1882 Reservation invaded and occupied by the Navajo graziers, but, in effect, this opposition denied historic Hopi usufruct claims to the lands in dispute and conceded control to the inimical Navajo! The practical effect of the intransigent stance of the extremist leadership was hardly consistent with its assertion that it represented the traditional Hopi way of life. As the extremist leadership multiplies such cases of discrepancy between its announced goals and the practical effect of its real actions, it alienates even traditionally-oriented Hopis who decide issues more on their merits than in terms of an almost automatic condemnation of any initiative not originating in the ranks of the extremist leadership itself.

Another debilitating influence upon the extremist leadership that appears certain to diminish its future influence is its continued search for the legendary White leader who will come to solve all Hopi problems. The not very discriminating quest for this leader has already led the extremist leadership into a costly dissipation of time and energy. It has brought certain traditionalist leaders into active association with socially marginal Whites, among them, those actively engaged in contacting flying saucers, or at least in obtaining the press publicity accorded such exotic activities.

The quest for the legendary White leader has also motivated certain of the traditionalist leaders to expend their energies in the almost aimless nihilism advocated by some "hippie" groups. This same yearning for a miraculous non-Hopi saviour has involved members of the extremist traditional leadership with a number of Whites marginal to their own society who have sought to exploit these Hopis for their own selfish ends in a fairly wide variety of ways. Such involvements not only dissipate the energies of the extremist leaders, but they also demonstrate to Hopis familiar with United States society as a whole that the path of extremism tends to lead Indian conservatives into social traps that are counterproductive even for dominant group members.

Tribal Council

The Hopi Tribal Council stands out in rather bold contrast to the increasingly futile leadership of traditionalist extremists. We anticipate that the Council will emerge with increasing authority as the major voice, truly representing the Hopis who choose to reside in the historic villages. This is not to say that the Council has been able to speak for all Hopis in the past, nor that its task has ever been or ever will be an easy one.

The moment it was established as an all-Hopi governing body, the Council suffered a severe handicap from the historic factionalism present within each pueblo, and the even more fundamental division between Hopi settlements. Each Pueblo in New Mexico historically has governed itself and been recognized as a sovereign entity by Spaniards and Anglo–Americans alike. The nature of Hopi pueblo governance differs little in terms of village autonomy from that of the New Mexican Pueblos. Thus, the organization of an all-Hopi Tribal Council, under the stimulus of the Indian Reorganization Act of 1934, flew in the face of centuries of customary political organization. Quite naturally, therefore, the all-Hopi Council has struggled mightily to speak for all villages. Nonetheless, we perceive a number of factors favoring that struggle now and in the predictable future.

One dynamic element in the situation stems from the socio-political position of the all-Hopi Council, the body of leaders recognized by the U. S. federal government as the only legal representative of all Hopis. This makes the all-Hopi Council the official buffer between dominant Anglo–American society and the Hopi people. It also inevitably provides the Tribal Council and its members with extensive patronage, which we expect to increase in the future as additional natural resources come under economic exploitation.

The present patronage power of the Tribal Council has not always existed. In fact, for perhaps a score of years after its initial organization, the lack of authority of that body stemmed quite directly from

Photograph by John Griffin

CONTEMPORARY AERIAL VIEW of First Mesa and its villages. Walpi perches on the far point; Sichomovi is in the center; and the Tewa pueblo of Hano is in the foreground.

its lack of patronage with which to motivate wide popular support. During the 1950s, however, the members of the Council began to execute agreements for the commercial exploitation of Reservation oil and mineral resources, over the vociferous objections of the "traditional Hopi chiefs" who clamored against any despoilation of the surface of Mother Earth. As commercial exploitation of tribally-owned resources commenced, the all-Hopi Tribal Council received royalty payments that provided it for the first time with significant economic resources. With millions of dollars at its command, the all-Hopi Tribal Council has been able to dispense patronage in the form of jobs with the Tribal government, and creation of industrial employment through such ventures as Tribal financing of a textile factory in nearby Winslow, dubious though the success of the industrial association with the BVD company proved to be.

In the future, then, we foresee the all-Hopi Tribal Council as gradually winning the leadership of all or nearly all of those Hopis who elect to remain residents of the reservation settlements and try to follow a traditional way of life. In other words, as the present extremist leadership literally dies out, many of its conservative functions will, we anticipate, necessarily gravitate to the Council. Thus, we expect that the future main division between Hopis will be that between reservation residents and migrants to ethnically mixed towns and cities outside the Reservation who more or less completely reject traditional life-style and economic pursuits.

In the all-important realm of the supernatural, we anticipate that the native Hopi religious leaders will in time reconcile their dogma with all-Hopi governance, unifying to a considerable degree behind the councilmen. One dynamic producing such a change is very likely to be an increasing abandonment of traditional Hopi beliefs by emigrants to the ethnically mixed settlements, as they join Christian denominations or fall into atheism or indifference.

The Hopi belief that a White leader will appear to lead the Hopi people into a better future will almost certainly continue to generate new factionalism, and new dissipations of Hopi energies as individuals and groups identify one or another White aberrant individual as the predicted Messiah. Experience should, however, make Hopis increasingly wary of the many false Messiahs who will assuredly present themselves.

Can a solution be found for these dilemmas that continue to confront the Hopi? Perhaps. To maintain their ethnic identity, the Hopi must continue to maintain their social structure and their ceremonial system. In these there is security and strength. To be realistic, all Hopi — traditionalist and progressive alike — must realize that change is not only inevitable, but is a dynamic characteristic of a living culture. As one student of the Hopi crisis remarked: "When the Hopi refuse to change — when they meet the new challenge by taking refuge in rigid and static tradition — their cultural doom is sealed." Hopis, to survive as Hopis, must maintain whatever they desire from their own culture, but they cannot be totally inflexible in their beliefs. At the same time, the more progressive elements need caution in discarding everything that smacks of Hopi traditionalism. All must have enough confidence in their own age-old strength to be able to adopt the best of the new without repudiating the important values of the old. Many Hopis, but unfortunately too few Whites, probably realize this. The best hope for future unity lies in these Hopis taking the lead in working out a practical program for using the foundation of Hopi culture upon which to build realistically in terms of today's world. Drawing the older, more traditional Hopi into a face-to-face dialogue about these problems may be more difficult, if not impossible, but it should be attempted. The great hope for the Hopi, however, will be the growing number of well-educated, world-traveled young Hopis who, with considerable perception of the "outside world" and the problems that it poses for their people, at the same time believe fervently in the Hopi way and participate fully in it. As one of these Hopis said not long ago: "The Hopi road is long, and strong, and endless."

SUGGESTED READING

THESE BOOKS CONTAIN firsthand accounts of the Hopi people at different times in their history and are reasonably accessible in major libraries, if not now in print. Shorter and more technical reports may be found in several scientific journals.

COLTON, HAROLD S. *Hopi Kachina Dolls*. Albuquerque: The University of New Mexico Press, 1949.

The most definite key to the identification of Hopi kachinas.

DOZIER, EDWARD P. *Hano, A Tewa Indian Community in Arizona*. New York: Holt, Rinehart, and Winston, Inc., 1966.

Paperback edition of the best study of the Tewa village on First Mesa.

_____. *The Pueblo Indians of North America*. New

York: Holt, Rinehart, and Winston, Inc., 1970.

A recently published comparative study of all Southwestern Pueblo Indians, including the Hopi.

EASTON, ROBERT and MACKENZIE BROWN. *Bullying the Moqui.* Prescott, Arizona: Prescott College Press, 1968.

An edited account of Indian agents' mistreatment of the Hopis at the opening of the 20th century.

GUMERMAN, GEORGE J. *Black Mesa: Surveys and Excavations in Northeastern Arizona, 1968.* Prescott, Arizona: Prescott College Press, 1968.

An up-to-date study of archaeological excavations in ruins of Hopi ancestors.

HACK, JOHN T. *The Changing Physical Environment of the Hopi Indians of Arizona.* Peabody Museum Papers No. 35:1. Cambridge: Harvard University Press, 1942.

An excellent geographic study of the Hopi mesas and environs.

HODGE, GENE MEANY. *The Kachinas Are Coming.* Flagstaff, Arizona: Northland Press, 1967.

A facsimile edition of this classic book of kachina dolls with related folktales.

Hopi History. Museum of Northern Arizona Reprint Series No. 2. Flagstaff, 1951.

Hopi Agriculture. Museum of Northern Arizona Reprint Series No. 5. Flagstaff, 1954.

Hopi Customs, Folklore and Ceremonies. Museum of Northern Arizona Reprint Series No. 4. Flagstaff, 1954.

Hopi Indian Arts and Crafts. Museum of Northern Arizona Reprint Series No. 3. Flagstaff, 1951.

Collected reports of years of Hopi research by associates of the Museum of Northern Arizona.

MONTGOMERY, ROSS G., WATSON SMITH and J. O. BREW. *Franciscan Awatovi: The Excavation and Conjectural Reconstruction of a 17th-Century Spanish Mission Establishment at a Hopi Indian Town in Northeastern Arizona.* Peabody Museum Papers No. 35. Cambridge: Harvard University Press, 1949.

A superb book on the archaeological excavation of 17th Century Awatovi.

SIMPSON, RUTH. *The Hopi Indians.* Southwest Museum Leaflet No. 25. Los Angeles, 1953.

A good summary account of historic Hopi culture.

SPICER, EDWARD H. *Cycles of Conquest: The Impact of Spain, Mexico, and the United States on the Indians of the Southwest, 1533–1960.* Tucson: The University of Arizona Press, 1962.

The finest ethnohistorical account ever produced of Southwestern Indians and their transculturation. Available in paperback.

THOMPSON, LAURA. *Culture in Crisis*. New York: Harper & Brothers, 1950.

Even though 20 years old, this remains the best treatment of contemporary Hopi problems and their solutions.

THOMPSON, LAURA and ALICE JOSEPH. *The Hopi Way*. Chicago: University of Chicago Press, 1944.

A good analysis of Hopi socialization and Hopi social and ceremonial organization.

TITIEV, MISCHA. *Old Oraibi*. Peabody Museum Papers 22:1. Harvard University, 1944.

An excellent ethnography of this centuries-old Third Mesa village.

WRIGHT, BARTON and EVELYN ROAT. *This is a Hopi Kachina*. Flagstaff, Arizona: Northland Press, 1970.

ROBERT C. EULER, Chairman of the Center for Man and Environment at Prescott College, is a former chairman of the Department of Anthropology at the University of Utah. Earlier he taught at Northern Arizona University at Flagstaff and at Wesleyan University in Wesleyan, Connecticut. A native of New York, Euler earned his Ph.D. degree from the University of New Mexico after obtaining the M.A. and B.A. degrees from Arizona State College. Euler has conducted anthropological research among the Havasupai, Hualapai, Hopi, and southern Paiute as well as with archaeological cultures in the Southwest.

HENRY F. DOBYNS, Professor of Anthropology at Prescott College, is a former professor and chairman of the Department of Anthropology at the University of Kentucky. Earlier he served as Lecturer and Senior Research Associate in the anthropology department at Cornell University, where he coordinated the Comparative Studies of Cultural Change and Andean Indian Community Research-and-Development (Ecuador, Peru, Bolivia) programs. A native of Arizona, Dobyns earned the B.A. and M.A. degrees from the University of Arizona, and the Ph.D. from Cornell. He conducted anthropological research for the Hualapai, Havasupai, Papago, and Pima tribes of Arizona.